Exploration & Encounters
1450–1550

The Search for the East

Peter Chrisp

Thomson Learning
New York

Exploration & Encounters 1450-1550
The Search for the East
Voyages to the New World
The Spanish Conquests in the New World
The Search for a Northern Route

Cover pictures: Ptolemy's world map, recreated in 1486; and a detail of a painting by Verbeek (1590-1635) of a Dutch merchantship in a storm.
Title page picture: A sixteenth-century engraving of a busy harbor.

First published in the United States in 1993 by
Thomson Learning
115 Fifth Avenue
New York, NY 10003

First published in 1993 by Wayland (Publishers) Ltd.

Cataloging-in-Publication Data applied for

ISBN: 1-56847-120-3

Printed in Italy

Picture acknowledgments

t = top   b = bottom   i = inset   l = left   r = right
The publishers would like to thank the following for permission to use their pictures in this book: Archiv für Kunst und Geschichte 12 (both), 13, 21, 26, 27, 33; Billie Love 22; Bridgeman Art Library 5 (t), 8, 16, 19, 40, 44; E.T. Archives Limited 9 (t), 11, 29, 30 (r), 41 (i); Link 25 (Dominic Muscat); Mary Evans title page, 5 (b), 6, 7 (i), 14, 15, 18, 23, 37, 38, 45; Fotomas Index 17 (t), 32, 39, 42, 43 (t); Michael Holford cover (both), 17 (l & r), 20, 34, 35, 42 (both); Photri 4; Wayland Picture Library 30 (l); Werner Forman Archive Limited 31, 36. The artwork was supplied by Mike Taylor.

SOURCES OF QUOTES
Page 6   C.W.R.D. Moseley (trans.), *The Travels of Sir John Mandeville* (Penguin Classics, 1983) p. 137.
Page 11   Luiz Vas de Camoens, *The Lusiads*, trans. W C. Atkinson, (Penguin Classics, 1952) p. 39.
Page 19   Gomes Eannes de Azurara, *Chronicle of the Discovery and Conquest of Guinea*, trans. C.R. Beazeley (Hakluyt Society, 1896) Vol. 1, p. 30.
Page 20   African oral account, quoted by C.R. Boxer, *The Portuguese Seaborn Empire* (Hutchinson, 1969), p. 102.
Page 21   G.R. Crone (ed. and trans.), *The Voyages of Cadamosto* (Hakluyt Society, 1937) pp. 20-21.
Page 23   Azurara, (trans.), *op. cit.*, Vol. 1, p. 81.
Page 27   Duarte Pacheco Pereira, *Esmeraldo de Situ Orbis*, ed. and trans. George Kimble (Hakluyt Society, 1936) p. 166.
Page 29   Quoted by David Simkin, *Voyages of Exploration* (Tressell, 1991) p. 31.
Page 33   Quoted by J.H. Parry, *The European Reconnaissance: Selected Documents* (Macmillan, 1968) p. 89.
Page 35   Quoted by J.H. Parry, *op. cit.*, p. 85.
Page 37   Gaspar Correa, *Lendas de India* (c. 1561), in *The Three Voyages of Vasco de Gama,* ed. and trans. Lord Stanley (Hakluyt Society, 1869) p. 331.
Page 39   Quoted by R.P. Rao, *Portuguese Rule in Goa* (Asia Publishing House, Delhi, 1963) p. 30.

CONTENTS

Europe in the Middle Ages

In the Middle Ages, the world known to Europeans was a tiny place. Travel was difficult and full of dangers, so most people rarely went farther than the nearest town.

Europeans knew about the lands around the Mediterranean Sea, such as North Africa and the Middle East, but they only had vague ideas of more distant countries.

For example, although they knew the North African coast, they had no idea how big Africa itself was or whether it was possible to sail around it.

One reason they knew so little was that North Africa and the Middle East were ruled by Muslims, followers of the religion of Islam. The people of Europe were mainly Christians, and they called their religion

This map shows the world known to Europeans before the voyages of exploration. They had no idea of the size or shape of Africa.

4

the "true faith." They believed that their own religion and way of life were better than all others, and they hated the Muslims, calling them the enemies of God. Throughout the Middle Ages, the Christians fought a series of wars against the Muslims, called the Crusades.

The hatred between the Christians and the Muslims made it very difficult for Europeans to travel by land into Africa or Asia. The Muslim lands were like a barrier, cutting Europe off from the wider world. (See map on page 7.)

In the fifteenth century, one European country, Portugal, found its way around the Muslim barrier by taking to the sea. This book is about the Portuguese voyages of exploration.

Above Christians believed that their holy city, Jerusalem, must be the center of the world.

Left Crusaders attack a Muslim city. Like these crusaders, the Portuguese explorers wanted to defeat the Muslims.

5

Travelers' Tales

Although most Europeans stayed at home, a few daring merchants and friars did travel overland to distant countries. Some of them returned and described the strange people and customs they had seen. When their stories were published in books, they were often full of wild exaggerations.

One of the most popular books of travelers' stories was *The Travels of Sir John Mandeville*, written in the 1350s: *In one isle, there is a race of giants, foul and horrible to look at. They have one eye only, in the middle of their foreheads . . . In another part, there are ugly folk without heads, who have eyes in each shoulder; their mouths are in the middle of their chests . . . There is still another isle where the people have only one foot, which is so broad that it will cover all the body and shade it from the sun. They will run so fast on this one foot that it is a marvel to see them.*

Europeans imagined that strange beings lived in distant lands.

6

One story which was often told was that, somewhere in Asia or Africa, there was a powerful Christian king called Prester John. Prester John was supposed to be extremely rich. It was said that he slept on a bed of gold set with precious stones, and that he was so important even his cooks and servants were kings in their own right.

At a time when the Muslims seemed so strong, Europeans eagerly listened to the stories of Prester John. If only the Christian rulers of Europe could find Prester John, they were sure he would help them in their wars against the Muslims. One reason for sending out voyages of exploration was to find Prester John.

The Muslim lands were like a barrier cutting off Europe from the wider world. The figure is Prester John, the legendary Christian king.

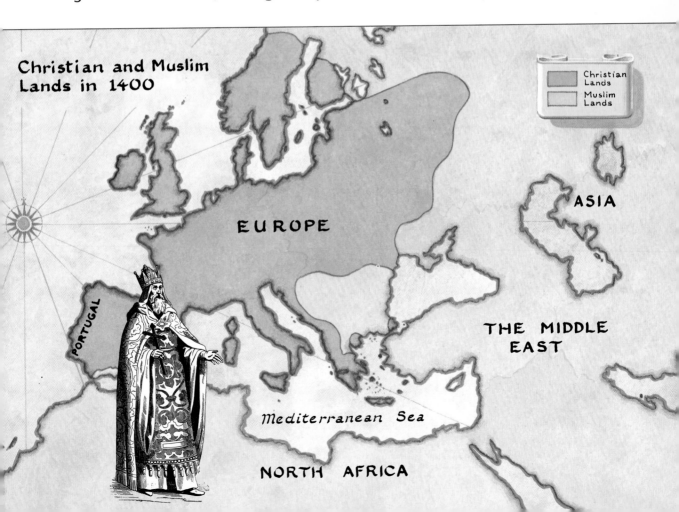

Christian and Muslim Lands in 1400

Christian Lands
Muslim Lands

ASIA

EUROPE

PORTUGAL

THE MIDDLE EAST

Mediterranean Sea

NORTH AFRICA

Gold and Spices

Europeans had practical reasons for wanting to reach distant lands. There were two things Europe lacked and desperately wanted – gold and spices.

People have always valued gold, a beautiful, rare metal that can be made into jewelry and coins. There was not much gold in Europe, but people knew there was a rich

A miser counts his gold coins. The Portuguese explorers dreamed of finding a land of gold in Africa.

source somewhere in Africa. They knew that Muslims brought gold dust across the Sahara to the North African markets.

Spices were worth even more than gold. In the Middle Ages, it was very difficult to keep meat fresh. People didn't have refrigerators. Most of the meat people ate was salted to preserve it or was either going rotten. Spices, such as pepper, could hide the taste of rotting or salted meat. They were also important as medicines. But spices were very scarce. They were brought from the Far East to Egypt by the

A fifteenth-century spice merchant.

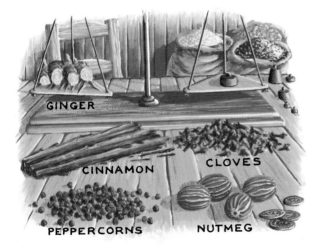

An illustration of some spices from the Far East.

Muslims, who made their fortunes selling spices to Italian merchants. The Italians made a big profit selling the spices to other Europeans.

If Europeans could have gone straight to the places that produced the gold and spices, they would not have had to pay the high prices charged by the Muslims.

Portugal

Portugal is a small country on the western edge of Europe. In 1400, fewer than a million people lived there. Most of these were poor farmers, trying to make a living from the rocky soil. Other European nations had more people and greater riches. However, it was the Portuguese who first sent out ships to find the gold of Africa and the spices of the East.

Unlike Spain, France, and Italy, Portugal did not have a port on the Mediterranean Sea. So the Portuguese had to look elsewhere for sea trade. Portugal's coastline faces the Atlantic Ocean. Here the winds and currents drive ships to the southwest – perfect for the exploration of Africa.

Portugal and its neighbors, showing the winds and currents of the Atlantic Ocean.

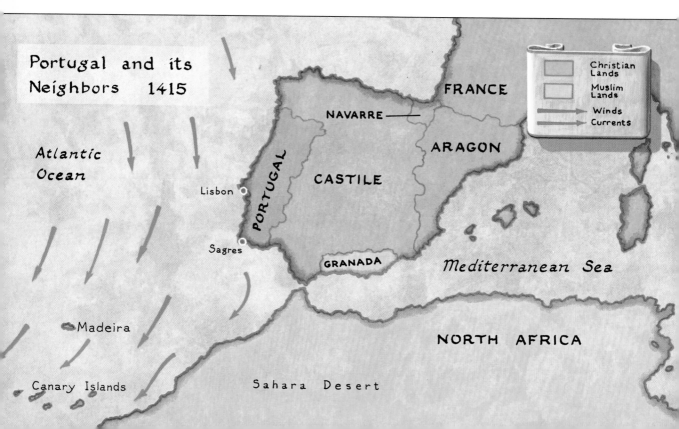

Portugal and its Neighbors 1415

Christian Lands
Muslim Lands
Winds
Currents

FRANCE
NAVARRE
ARAGON
CASTILE
PORTUGAL
Lisbon
Sagres
GRANADA
Atlantic Ocean
Mediterranean Sea
Madeira
Canary Islands
Sahara Desert
NORTH AFRICA

A bustling harbor scene with a ship getting ready to sail.

Luiz Vaz de Camões (1524-80) is a famous Portuguese poet. He wrote a great poem about the Portuguese explorers of the fifteenth century. It begins like this:

This is the story of heroes who, leaving their native Portugal behind them, opened a way to Ceylon, and further, across seas no man had ever sailed before. They were men of no ordinary sort, equally at home in war and in dangers of every kind: they founded a new kingdom among distant peoples, and made it great.

Portugal had a long history of fighting against the Muslims. The Portuguese nobles were proud and warlike, and eager to show their bravery. One way they could do this would be to lead expeditions into unknown seas. They saw themselves as daring knights and their voyages as heroic quests.

Henry the Navigator

It was thanks to Prince Henry, a younger son of King John I, that the Portuguese began to send ships to explore the unknown seas. Henry has been nicknamed "the Navigator" (sea explorer), although he never went on a voyage of exploration himself. But he did more than any other person to make the voyages possible.

Prince Henrique of Portugal, better known as Henry the Navigator.

A fifteenth-century globe, showing the discoveries made by Prince Henry's captains. This is the oldest globe in existence.

In 1419, Henry was made the governor of the Algarve, the southernmost part of Portugal. From his headquarters at Sagres, he sent ships to explore the Atlantic and the coast of Africa. They were commanded by nobles from his household.

At Sagres, scientists and sea captains could meet to swap knowledge about the design of ships and new ways of finding direction at sea. Here also maps were made, using the information brought back by the sailors.

The Prince had several reasons for sending out voyages. His greatest wish was to launch a new crusade and drive the Muslims from North Africa. In Africa, he hoped to find Christian rulers, who would help him in this crusade. At the same time, he wanted to strike a blow against the Muslims by seizing their trade. The gold of Africa would make Portugal rich and powerful.

Henry admires the work of his mapmakers, in his headquarters at Sagres.

The Portuguese Caravels

In the early fifteenth century, the Portuguese developed a new kind of sailing ship called a caravel. It was small and

A caravel with its lateen sails.

light, and it usually had lateen (triangular) sails. It was better than any other European ship of the time for voyages of exploration.

In northern Europe, sailors went to sea in tublike ships with square sails. Their round bellies sat deep in the water, which made them stable but slow. Such ships were no good for exploring unfamiliar coastlines, where they ran the risk of going aground in shallow water.

Meanwhile, in the Mediterranean the favorite ships were galleys – ships powered by oars. These needed a large crew of oarsmen who all had to be fed. They could not travel far without taking on supplies.

Mediterranean galleys, powered by dozens of oars, were not suitable for long voyages of exploration.

Unlike the northern ships, the new caravels were fast and light; unlike the galleys, they needed only a small crew. Their greatest feature was their lateen sails. No sailing vessel can sail straight into the wind. It has to tack – move from side to side in a zigzag line. A ship with triangular sails is much better at tacking than one with square sails. Caravels could sail down the coast of northwest Africa with the wind behind them, and then tack back home against the wind.

By modern standards, caravels were cramped and uncomfortable. There were no sleeping quarters, so the sailors had to sleep on the open decks. Yet the tiny caravels were home to the crews for weeks on end.

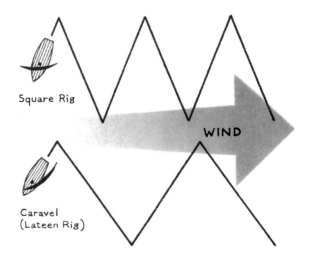

Thanks to its lateen sails, the caravel was much better at sailing into the wind. The square rig (top) has to tack five times, the caravel (bottom) only three.

Finding the Way at Sea

An early navigator (left) finds the way by using an astrolabe. This was a tricky operation on the rolling deck of a ship.

On their voyages of exploration, the Portuguese caravels would often be sailing in the open sea, with no landmarks to guide them. The sea captains had to learn new methods of navigation – the skill of finding the way at sea.

The most important skill was dead reckoning. That meant using the speed of the ship and the direction it was traveling to figure out its location. Speed was found by dropping wood chips overboard and then seeing how long it took for the ship to pass them. Direction was found using a compass. The navigator would then draw a line on his chart showing the course he thought the ship had traveled.

Navigators could work out their latitude (position to the north or south) by looking at the North Star or the midday sun. These appear at different heights in the sky at different latitudes. By measuring the sun's height above the horizon, sailors could find how far south they had traveled.

Below An astrolabe.

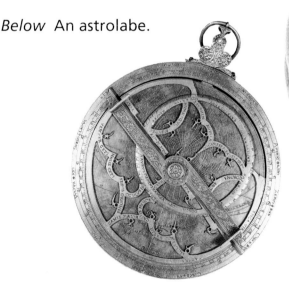

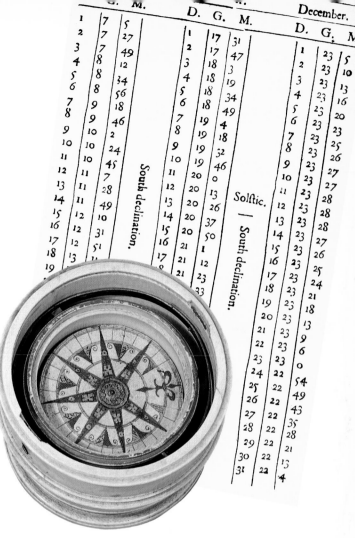

The table on the right shows the sun's position:

D. G. M.	South declination		D. G. M.	Solftic. — South declination		December. D. G. M.		
1	7	5	1	17	31	1	23	5
2	7	27	2	17	47	2	23	10
3	7	49	3	18	3	3	23	13
4	8	12	4	18	19	4	23	16
5	8	34	5	18	34	5	23	20
6	8	56	6	18	49	6	23	23
7	9	18	7	19	4	7	23	25
8	9	46	8	19	18	8	23	26
9	10	2	9	19	32	9	23	27
10	10	24	10	19	46	10	23	27
11	10	45	11	20	0	11	23	28
12	11	7	12	20	13	12	23	28
13	11	28	13	20	26	13	23	28
14	11	49	14	20	37	14	23	27
15	12	10	15	20	50	15	23	26
16	12	31	16	21	1	16	23	25
17	12	51	17	21	12	17	23	24
18	13			21	23	18	23	21
19					33	19	23	18
						20	23	13
						21	23	9
						22	23	6
						23	23	0
						24	22	54
						25	22	49
						26	22	43
						27	22	35
						28	22	28
						29	22	21
						30	22	13
						31	22	4

Above A magnetic compass, and a set of tables showing the sun's position at various latitudes.

At first they did this just by holding up a lance and squinting at the sun. By the 1460s they were using special instruments called the quadrant and the astrolabe to find out their latitude. In 1478, Portuguese astronomer Abraham Zacuto published a set of tables showing the sun's position at different latitudes. With an astrolabe and Zacuto's tables, navigators could find their latitude quickly and more accurately than before.

Fears of the Southern Sea

One big problem in exploration was fear of the unknown. Europeans knew that lands to the south were hotter than their own. Many thought that if they sailed too far south they would reach a place so hot that the sea would boil and steam and the land would be scorched. No human being could survive in such heat. Who knew what kinds of monsters might live there?

Portuguese sailors were also superstitious about the west coast of Africa, with its strong winds and currents. They said that no ship could sail past a certain point called Cape Bojador and get back home again.

Early sailors were terrified of sea monsters.

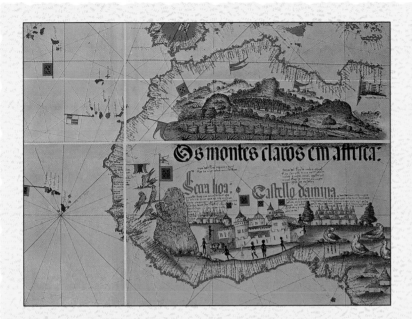

A map of the west coast of Africa, with the Portuguese names given by Henry's captains.

Gomez Eannes de Azurara wrote this about Cape Bojador:

Although Prince Henry sent out many ships, not one dared to pass Cape Bojador and learn about the land that lay beyond it. This was because of the newness of the idea and the widespread and ancient rumor about this Cape . . . For, said the sailors, this much is clear, beyond this Cape there are no men. The land there is like the deserts of Libya, with no water or plants . . . The currents there are so terrible that no ship having once passed the Cape will ever be able to return.

For twelve years, Prince Henry sent out ships with orders to sail past Cape Bojador. But as soon as the sailors saw the low-lying headland, they would panic and demand to turn back. Finally, in 1434, the cape was rounded by a captain called Gil Eannes. It was his second try, and he sailed only far enough to say that he had done it.

The Portuguese in West Africa

As they edged their way down the west coast of Africa, the Portuguese came into contact with many different peoples. The appearance and customs of these peoples seemed very strange to the explorers. In the same way, the Africans were amazed at the sight of the white men in their ships.

To the Africans, the Portuguese seemed like beings from another world. This African carving shows Portuguese figures supporting a ship.

A captain called Alvise de Cadamosto, who explored West Africa in 1455, described the reaction of the Africans to the Portuguese ships and sailors that landed:

It is said that the first time they saw sails . . . they believed they were great seabirds with white wings, which were flying and had come from some strange place . . . Some thought the ships were fishes, others that they were ghosts that went by night, at which they were terrified . . .

These negroes crowded to see me as though I were a marvel. Some touched my hands and limbs, and rubbed me with their spit to see whether my whiteness was dye or flesh. Finding that it was flesh, they were amazed . . .

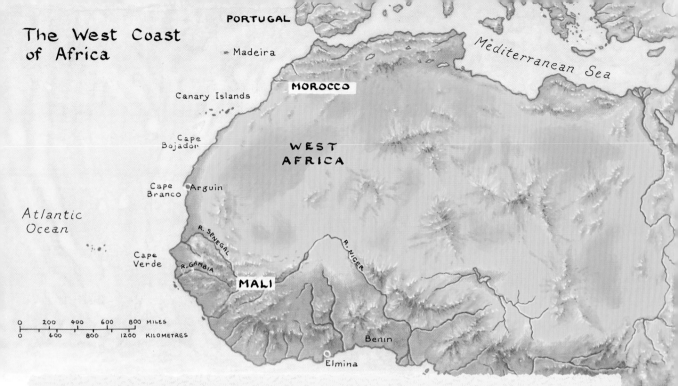

The West Coast of Africa

PORTUGAL

Madeira

Mediterranean Sea

Canary Islands

MOROCCO

Cape Bojador

WEST AFRICA

Cape Branco • Arguin

Atlantic Ocean

R. SENEGAL

Cape Verde

R. GAMBIA

R. NIGER

MALI

| 0 | 200 | 400 | 600 | 800 MILES |
| 0 | 400 | 800 | 1200 | KILOMETRES |

Benin

Elmina

A Portuguese soldier, cast in bronze, made in Benin, West Africa.

Unlike the Portuguese, the Africans did not write their history. They remembered past events through storytelling. This is how the Pende people recalled the coming of the Portuguese with their ships and guns:

One day the white men arrived in ships with wings, which shone in the sun like knives. They fought hard battles with the Ngola (chief) and spat fire at him . . . The white men came yet again . . . From that time until our day, the whites brought us nothing but wars and miseries.

21

Slaves

In the 1440s, the Portuguese began to capture Africans from their villages. At first, they did this to learn about the country. But they soon realized that they could make a lot of money by selling the Africans as slaves back in Portugal.

At the time, Europeans thought that there was nothing wrong with forcing people into

Men trading a slave. The Portuguese did not introduce slavery to Africa, but they practiced it on a much greater scale than the Africans had.

slavery, as long as they were not Christians. They argued that slavery would be a first step to teaching people the "true faith." The slaves might lose their freedom, but their souls would be saved.

In the African villages, word soon spread that the white men were taking people away in their ships. Many believed that the strangers were taking the people in order to kill and eat them. The Africans fought back. In 1446, twenty sailors were killed by poison arrows while raiding a village. The Portuguese realized that it was easier to trade for slaves with local chiefs rather than capture them themselves. These chiefs had slaves of their own, and would sell them for European goods.

The writer Azurara watched the first big shipload of slaves arrive in Portugal in 1444: *Some kept their heads low and their faces bathed in tears, looking at each other . . . others struck themselves in the face and threw themselves to the ground; and others sang sad songs – although we did not understand their words, the sound told of their great sorrow.*

It was necessary to separate them, fathers from sons, husbands from wives, brothers from brothers . . . The mothers threw themselves flat on the ground. They were beaten but they refused to give up their children.

The slave trade started by the Portuguese would last for 400 years. This nineteenth-century engraving comes from the time when some Europeans began to argue that slavery was an evil thing.

The Rounding of the Cape

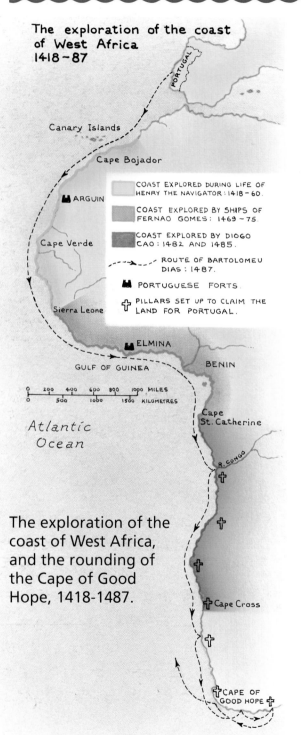

The exploration of the coast of West Africa 1418–87

COAST EXPLORED DURING LIFE OF HENRY THE NAVIGATOR: 1418–60.

COAST EXPLORED BY SHIPS OF FERNAO GOMES: 1469–75.

COAST EXPLORED BY DIOGO CAO: 1482 AND 1485.

- - - → ROUTE OF BARTOLOMEU DIAS: 1487.

PORTUGUESE FORTS.

✝ PILLARS SET UP TO CLAIM THE LAND FOR PORTUGAL.

Canary Islands

Cape Bojador

ARGUIN

Cape Verde

Sierra Leone

ELMINA

GULF OF GUINEA

BENIN

0   200   400   600   800   1000 MILES
0   500   1000   1500 KILOMETRES

Atlantic Ocean

Cape St. Catherine

R. CONGO ✝

✝

✝

✝ Cape Cross

✝

✝ CAPE OF GOOD HOPE ✝

PORTUGAL

The exploration of the coast of West Africa, and the rounding of the Cape of Good Hope, 1418-1487.

Prince Henry died in 1460, but the voyages of exploration carried on without him. They were now bringing back a profit in slaves, ivory (the beautiful, white horn of elephants' tusks), and gold dust. The explorers also saw that the African coast swung sharply to the east. There seemed a real chance that India, with its rich spice markets, might be just around the corner. In fact, they had still only gotten about halfway down the west of Africa.

In the 1470s, a wealthy merchant called Fernao Gomes paid for a series of voyages along the coast. His captains were disappointed to find the coastline swinging down to the south. The new king, John II, then became interested in the voyages. In 1482 he sent an explorer

This mural remembers Dias's landing in southern Africa. It shows his men putting up a stone cross on the shore.

called Diogo Cao to find the sea route to India. Cao made two voyages. He traveled another 1,450 miles around Africa. His voyages showed that Africa was much bigger than anyone had expected.

Bartolomeu Dias was the next explorer to be sent. In 1487, his caravels fought their way south against strong winds and currents. For two weeks a fierce storm drove him out of sight of land. Then, sailing north, he sighted the coast on his left side instead of on his right. He had sailed around the southern tip of Africa without realizing it. The cape (or tip of land) he found was named the Cape of Good Hope – for now the way to India lay open.

The Expedition to India

In 1497, King Manuel of Portugal organized an expedition to sail to India. It was led by a thirty-six-year-old nobleman called Vasco da Gama.

Careful preparations were made. Four ships were readied, including a caravel and a store ship. The two other ships were specially built for the voyage. They were bigger and stronger than caravels, and they carried square sails, which were easier to handle in rough weather than the caravels' lateen sails. Dias had found that caravels suffered badly from the storms of the south Atlantic.

The ships were loaded with enough food and drink to last three years. The crew of 170 men included a little group of convicts sent to do any dangerous jobs on land.

Da Gama took small samples of spices to show to the peoples he met, in the hope that they might tell him where these goods could be found.

Da Gama also carried a letter from the king to give to Prester John, the legendary

Vasco da Gama, who was chosen to lead the expedition to India.

Christian ruler. Although he had not been found in West Africa, the Portuguese still thought Prester John might be in East Africa or India.

In July 1497, the small fleet set sail for the East.

A writer and sea captain called Pacheco Pereira described the preparations:

The ships were built by excellent masters and workmen. Each had three sets of sails and anchors . . . The casks of wine, water, vinegar, and oil were strengthened with many hoops of iron. The supply of bread, wine, flour, meat, vegetables, and likewise of weapons and ammunition, were also more than was needed for such a voyage. The best and most skillful pilots and sailors were sent on this voyage. The money spent on the few ships was so great that I will not go into detail for fear of not being believed.

Vasco da Gama's flagship, the St. Gabriel, with its square sails.

Through the Atlantic

Instead of staying near the coast of Africa, as Dias had done, Vasco da Gama sailed out into the Atlantic Ocean. He wanted to use the south Atlantic winds, which blow in a huge circle. Dias had to fight against the wind almost all the way, but da Gama would have the wind behind him.

This was a daring move. It meant that the ships spent three months in the open sea, the longest time that any seafarers had been out of sight of land. As they were swept to the southwest, the sailors anxiously waited for a wind to take them back toward the coast of Africa.

A map showing Vasco da Gama's route to India, 1497-1498.

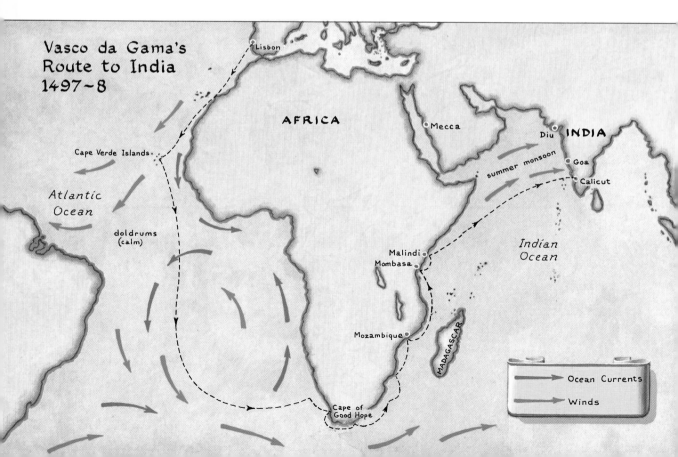

At last, they found a wind blowing toward the east and, at the beginning of November, they saw the south coast of Africa. The crews celebrated by putting on their best clothes, decorating their ships with flags, and firing their cannons in salute.

Although the explorers found none of the sea monsters they feared, they saw some things that seemed just as strange – such as flying fish.

Being out in the open sea, the ships could not take on fresh fruit and vegetables. The sailors began to suffer from scurvy, a disease caused by lack of vitamin C. Half of the men were to die of this. This is how one crew member described scurvy in his diary:

It rotted all my gums, which gave out a stinking black blood. My thighs and lower legs were also black and turning rotten and I was forced to use my knife each day to cut into the flesh to let out this black and foul blood. I also used my knife on my gums, which were turning black and blue and growing over my teeth.

When I had cut away this dead flesh, which caused much blood to flow, I rinsed my mouth and teeth with urine, rubbing them very hard.

Across the Indian Ocean

Vasco da Gama's fleet rounded the Cape of Good Hope and sailed on into the Indian Ocean. This ocean was new to Europeans, but Muslims had sailed it for centuries. They made use of the monsoons – winds that blow to the north-east in summer and then in the opposite direction in winter.

A mid-sixteenth-century map, showing the Indian Ocean, the east coast of Africa, and the west coast of India.

Da Gama's flagship was unlike anything that had sailed into an East African port before.

Traders would sail from Africa to India with the summer monsoon, carrying ivory and gold. In the autumn they would return with cotton and spices.

One of the aims of the Portuguese explorers was to spread the Christian faith. After da Gama's visit to Malindi, other Portuguese sailors stopped off there and built this small church.

Along the East African coast there were several Muslim cities that had grown rich from this trade.

The first city the Portuguese visited was Mozambique. The people welcomed the visitors, thinking they were Muslims who had come from a distant land. They stopped being friendly when da Gama explained that they were Christians, looking for the way to India. They would not help him, and neither would the people of Mombasa, farther up the coast.

In Malindi, the Portuguese finally met a ruler who was willing to help. He offered da Gama the services of one of his own pilots, who would show the way to India. The fleet sailed off.

On May 18, 1498, the ships sighted mountains on the horizon. They had been away from Portugal for nearly a year, but at last the search for the East was over.

Calicut

On May 21, the ships anchored off Calicut, one of the busiest ports on the Indian coast. Da Gama sent one of his convicts ashore to find out how the Portuguese would be greeted. He was met by two Muslim merchants from North Africa, who spoke Spanish. They were not pleased to hear the sailors had come in search of Christians and spices. They controlled the spice trade and they did not want any outsiders taking a share.

The ruler of Calicut, known as the Zamorin, agreed to meet da Gama, who came ashore with his men. They were led through streets packed with curious onlookers and taken to the royal palace. Here they found the Zamorin, lying on a green velvet couch.

The Zamorin welcomed the Portuguese politely. They were offered bananas, which they had never seen before and which they liked greatly. Da Gama explained that he had been sent by a distant and

Vasco da Gama's Portuguese clothes and massive beard must have looked strange to the people of Calicut.

powerful king to make a treaty of friendship and to look for trade. The Zamorin was not very impressed with the Portuguese – they had brought no expensive gifts. But he gave da Gama a letter for King Manuel.

Indian rulers expected foreign visitors to bring rich presents with them, but Vasco da Gama did not know this. A member of the crew described da Gama's gifts:
The captain got ready the following things to be sent to the Zamorin – four scarlet hoods, six hats, four strings of coral, a case of sugar, two casks of oil, and two of honey. When the Zamorin's officers saw the present they laughed at it, saying it was not a thing to offer to a Zamorin.

Da Gama is greeted by the Zamorin, who eyes him curiously.

Hindus or Christians?

In the fifteenth century, India was not a single country. It was a land made up of many different states. Some of the Indians were Muslims, while others were Hindus. The Hindus worshipped dozens of gods. Their temples were full of colorful images of their gods, often decorated with gold and jewels. The Zamorin and most of the people of Calicut were Hindus.

The Portuguese had never heard of Hindus. They had come expecting to find Christians in India. They could see that the people of Calicut had pictures in their temples. Muslims did not worship

A vast Hindu temple, built in the eleventh century. Hindu rulers built such large temples to show their wealth and power.

images, so they could not be Muslim. However, Christian churches did have images, of Christ and the saints. The Portuguese decided that the people of Calicut must be Christians. The Hindu ceremonies seemed odd, but the Portuguese put this down to the Indians not having been taught the "true faith" properly.

When Vasco da Gama returned to Portugal, he was given a hero's welcome. His mission was seen as a complete success. He had brought back samples of precious spices – pepper,

cinnamon, cloves, ginger, and nutmeg – and he had news of the "Christians" of India.

A bronze statuette of a Hindu goddess. Da Gama and his men thought that such images were of Christian saints.

 In his diary, a member of da Gama's expedition described a visit to a Hindu temple:

They threw holy water over us, and gave us some white earth, which the Christians of this country are in the habit of putting on their foreheads, breasts, around the neck, and on the forearms . . .

Many saints were painted on the walls of their church, wearing crowns. They were painted in different ways with teeth sticking out an inch below the mouth, and four or five arms.

War with the Muslims

Da Gama's route to India was quickly retraced. On March 9, 1500, six months after da Gama's return, Pedro Cabral set off with thirteen well-armed ships. When they arrived at Calicut, the Muslim merchants tried to stop the Portuguese from trading for spices. Cabral replied by bombarding the town with cannon fire. He returned to Portugal with ships packed with spices – as well as the news that the Hindus were not Christian after all.

Vasco da Gama made a second voyage to Calicut in 1502. On the way, he captured a Muslim ship carrying pilgrims back to India from the holy city of Mecca. He had all of them killed. Off Calicut, he overtook some fishing boats and again killed the people on board.

Above A Muslim Indian image of Portuguese soldiers – brutal and terrifying figures. The artist had a strange idea of European ships.

Right Calicut, stormed in 1509, became a Portuguese settlement.

Gaspar Correa, who knew da Gama, described what happened to some fishing boats, which da Gama found off Calicut in 1502:

Then the captain-major commanded them to cut off the hands and ears and noses of all the crews . . . and they were thus put on board, heaped upon the top of each other, mixed up with the blood which streamed from them; and he ordered mats and dry leaves to be spread over them, and the sails to be set for the shore, and the vessel set on fire . . .

Da Gama planned to spread terror along the Indian coast. He wanted the Muslim merchants to be too scared to put to sea. He hoped that the Hindu rulers of the coast would be frightened into letting the Portuguese build forts and trading bases in their cities. Like most Europeans of the time, da Gama thought there was nothing wrong with killing people who were not Christians.

From then on, there would be a bloody war between the Portuguese and the Muslims in the Indian Ocean.

A Sea Empire

Over the next few years, the Portuguese sent every available ship and soldier to fight in the Indian Ocean. In 1505, Francisco de Almeida

Afonso de Albuquerque was the most successful of the Portuguese commanders in seizing control in the Indian Ocean.

sailed up the East African coast with a powerful fleet of 22 ships and 1,500 soldiers. At each African city he visited, Almeida demanded that the ruler become a vassal of the Portuguese king. This meant the ruler had to obey the king's orders and pay a sum of money, called tribute, to him. If the ruler refused, his city would be attacked.

The Muslims of Egypt sent a fleet of war galleys to fight Almeida, but these were no match for the Portuguese ships. Galleys could not carry many guns, but relied on ramming enemy ships. This made them easy targets for the Portuguese cannon. In 1509, the Muslim fleet was destroyed in a sea battle at Diu.

The greatest Portuguese commander was Afonso de Albuquerque. In 1510, he

Goa became the most important Portuguese settlement in India. Here Portuguese settlers stroll through the streets of Goa.

seized Goa, the richest port on the Indian coast. This became the Portuguese capital in the Indian Ocean. With control of a few key ports and a powerful fleet, the Portuguese ruled the Indian Ocean. Any foreign ship they came across had to pay them tribute money, or it would be sunk.

The Portuguese had conquered an empire.

Albuquerque described the capture of Goa in a letter to the king of Portugal:

I then burned the city and put everything to the sword, and for days continuously the people shed blood. Wherever they were found and caught, no life was spared to any Muslim, and their mosques were filled up and set on fire. We counted 6,000 dead bodies. It was, my lord, a great deed, well fought and well finished. November 25, 1510

On to the Spice Islands

The Portuguese soon found that, apart from pepper, most of the spices sold in India did not originally come from there. The most valuable spices – cloves, mace, and nutmeg – came from some islands thousands of miles farther east. They became known as the Spice Islands.

Ships that traveled from India to the Spice Islands had to pass through a strait (a passage of water) between Sumatra and Malaya. The rich Muslim port of Malacca overlooked the strait. Albuquerque knew that if he could capture Malacca, he would be able to control all the trade between the Spice Islands and the West. In 1511, he led a war fleet to Malacca. Although he had only 1,100 men and the Malaccans had 30,000 soldiers, the Portuguese captured the port in nine days of fierce fighting.

Merchant ships load up with spices and silk in the Gulf of Cambay in northwest India.

From Malacca, Albuquerque sent three ships to explore the Spice Islands. They were guided on their voyage by pilots from Java. The ships reached the Banda Islands, which produced nutmeg and mace. A few years later, Portuguese ships reached the Moluccas, five tiny islands where cloves grew. On one of these islands, called Ternate, the Portuguese built a fortress.

The Portuguese now had all the spices their ships could carry. They began to search for other nearby lands where they could sell these goods.

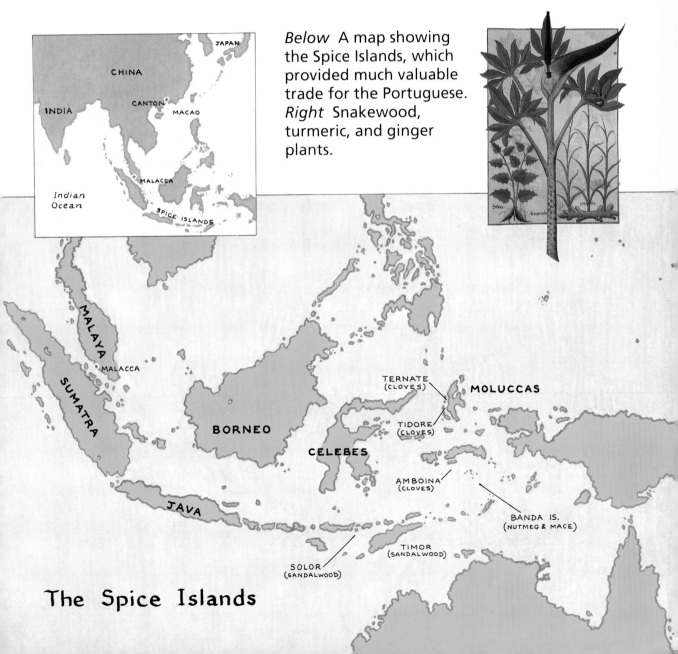

Below A map showing the Spice Islands, which provided much valuable trade for the Portuguese. *Right* Snakewood, turmeric, and ginger plants.

JAPAN

CHINA

CANTON

MACAO

INDIA

MALACCA

Indian Ocean

SPICE ISLANDS

MALAYA

MALACCA

SUMATRA

BORNEO

CELEBES

TERNATE (CLOVES)

MOLUCCAS

TIDORE (CLOVES)

AMBOINA (CLOVES)

BANDA IS. (NUTMEG & MACE)

JAVA

TIMOR (SANDALWOOD)

SOLOR (SANDALWOOD)

The Spice Islands

The Portuguese in China

The Portuguese now began to look toward China as a country they could trade with. In 1514, Portuguese merchants first arrived at the harbor of Canton on the coast of China. They did not know it, but they had reached a vast and powerful empire with one of the oldest civilizations in the world.

Like the Europeans, the Chinese believed that their own way of life was better than any other. At first they did not know what to make of the foreigners. In 1519, the Portuguese forced some Chinese into slavery and started building a fort on the Chinese coast. The Chinese were horrified, and they drove the foreigners out.

Portuguese ships anchor in the Chinese harbor of Canton, where they had come hoping to trade for silk and porcelain.

A procession by the Chinese governor of Macau, where the Portuguese were allowed to set up their trading base.

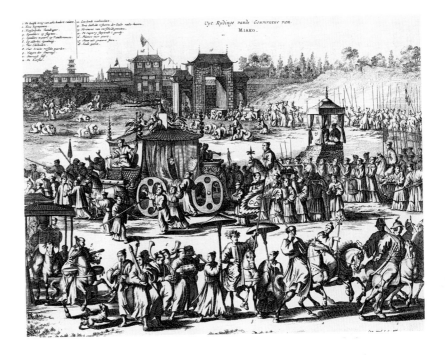

A law was passed that any ship reaching China with a *fan kwei* ("foreign devil") on board would be seized. A notice was painted in golden letters on the gates of Canton. It warned "the men with the beards and the large eyes" not to set foot on Chinese soil.

Although they were unwelcome on the mainland, in the 1550s the Portuguese were allowed to set up a

The Chinese were famous for their delicately painted ceramics.

trading base on the island of Macau, close to Canton. Each year a ship carrying European glassware and cloth and Indian cotton and spices would sail from Goa to Macau. Here it would take on Chinese silks and porcelain and then sail to Japan to trade for silver. The Portuguese had become successful worldwide traders.

The Age of Exploration

In the early sixteenth century Portugal was one of the most powerful countries in the world. The Portuguese controlled many places on the coast of Africa, dozens of distant settlements from India to the Spice Islands, and much of the Brazilian coast of South America.

When other European countries saw the riches that the Portuguese were bringing back from overseas, they decided that they wanted a share. Like the Portuguese, these other European nations believed that they had a right to take over foreign lands. The Spanish, the Dutch, the

Portuguese warships anchored off northern India. They were strong enough to defeat Muslim galleys, but they would soon have to fight against other Europeans, whose ships were also armed with powerful cannon.

44

The greatest threat to the Portuguese came from the Dutch, shown here attacking Malacca in 1606. The city finally fell to the Dutch in 1641.

English, and the French all sent out ships to find new routes to the East. European ships were soon sailing in all the world's oceans. The explorers claimed the lands they found for their own countries and gave these lands European names. Slowly, they put together a more accurate map of the world.

The Portuguese always had to fight to defend their settlements – their greed and cruelty made them many enemies. But now they had to fight fellow Europeans as well, people who were as well-armed and as ruthless as themselves.

There were too few Portuguese to protect their many settlements. It was said that God had given the Portuguese a tiny country to live in, but all the world to die in. Every year, about 2,400 men left Portugal for the overseas empire. Many died on the long voyage to India, others died of disease in the hot climates. With so few soldiers, the Portuguese gradually lost their control of the spice trade and much of their empire.

GLOSSARY

Astrolabe An instrument for finding latitude (position north or south) by measuring the height of the midday sun or the North Star at night. It is a brass disk with a rotating pointer that is aimed at the sun.

Caravel A Portuguese ship with lateen (triangular) sails, first used in the early 1400s.

Christian A follower of Christianity, the religion started in the first century by Jesus Christ. Christians believe that there is one god and that Jesus is god in human form.

Compass An instrument for finding direction. It uses a magnetic needle that always points north.

Crusades The Christian holy wars fought during the eleventh to the thirteenth centuries, mostly against Muslims in the Middle East.

Dead reckoning A way of working out a ship's position by recording and comparing its speed and direction.

Empire A group of countries or peoples ruled by a single state.

Exploration The search for unknown lands or new routes to known lands.

Friar A member of a Christian brotherhood. Friars traveled from place to place preaching their religion.

Galley A ship powered by oars, used in the Mediterranean Sea.

Hindu A follower of Hinduism, the ancient religion of India. Hindus worship many gods.

Lateen A triangular sail.

Latitude Position to the north or south of the equator (the imaginary line around the middle of the earth). Position to the east or west of a given point is called longitude.

Merchant Someone who buys and sells for a living, often by taking goods from one place to another.

Middle Ages Term used by historians to describe a period in European history, roughly between A.D. 1000 and 1500.

Muslim A follower of Islam, the religion started by Muhammad in the seventh century.

Muslims believe that there is one god and that Muhammad is god's messenger.

Navigation The science of finding the way from one place to another.

Quadrant An instrument for finding position to the north or south by measuring the height of the North Star or midday sun. The first quadrants were shaped like a quarter of a circle with a scale marked on the curved edge. A weighted line hung down from the corner. The navigator would point the straight edge at the star or sun, and then notice the position on the scale touched by the line.

Scurvy A disease caused by lack of vitamin C, once common on long voyages when supplies of fresh food, especially fruit, ran out.

Spices The seeds, leaves, or bark of certain plants that grow in hot climates and give flavor to food. Examples are pepper, cinnamon, cloves, and nutmeg.

Strait A narrow passage of water through land that joins two large areas of water.

Tribute Money or goods that powerful people force those who are less powerful to pay to them. Ships and cities in the Indian Ocean had to pay tribute to the Portuguese.

BOOKS TO READ

Asimov, Isaac. *Isaac Asimov's Pioneers of Science and Exploration.* 3 vols. Milwaukee: Gareth Stevens, 1991.

Grant, Neil. *The Great Atlas of Discovery.* New York: Knopf Books for Young Readers, 1992.

Hargrove, Jim. *Ferdinand Magellan: First Around the World.* The World's Great Explorers. Chicago: Childrens Press, 1990.

Humble, Richard. *The Travels of Marco Polo.* Exploration Through The Ages. New York: Franklin Watts, 1990.

Humble, Richard. *Vasco da Gama.* Exploration Through the Ages. New York: Franklin Watts, 1992.

Kent, Zachary. *Christopher Columbus: Expeditions to the New World.* The World's Great Explorers. Chicago: Childrens Press, 1991.

INDEX

Numbers in **bold** refer to illustrations as well as text.